QUESTIONS:

1. What is the capital city of Idaho?
2. What is the state bird of Alabama?
3. What is the state flower of Illinois?
4. Helen Keller's birthplace is in what state?
5. Which state is nicknamed the Hoosier State?
6. Name the 49th state.
7. Which state has the second longest coastline?
8. What is the name of the famous landmark in New York City which has 168 steps to its crown?

QUESTIONS:

1. Name the 48th state in the union.
2. Which state was previously known as Franklin, named for Benjamin Franklin?
3. Which state is nicknamed the Empire State?
4. "Home On The Range" is the state song for what midwestern state?
5. New Connecticut is the previous name of the only New England state without a seacoast. Name this state.
6. Which U.S. state has the longest coastline?
7. Which state is nicknamed the Golden State?
8. Which state still reserves the right to divide itself into *five* states if it so desires?

QUESTIONS:

1. Name two of the four state capitals named after U.S. Presidents.
2. Which two states do not have state songs?
3. Which state is nicknamed the Wolverine State?
4. Name the 50th state in the union.
5. The first recording to sell a *million* copies was Alma Gluck's version of what 1915 song about a southern state?
6. Alphabetically, what is the last state capital?
7. What was the first state to abolish slavery in 1780?
8. What is the only state song taken from a Broadway play?

QUESTIONS:

1. Which state is nicknamed the Show Me State?
2. Which state has no official nickname?
3. The only diamond mine in North America is located in what state?
4. What is California's state song?
5. Name two of the eight states that border Missouri.
6. What state uses "Yankee Doodle" as its official state song?
7. Which state was named after Admiral/Sir William Penn?
8. Which state is nicknamed the Sunshine State?

5 QUESTIONS:

1. The state bird of Maryland has the same name as a famous baseball team. What is it?
2. Which state is nicknamed the Bluegrass State?
3. What is the capital of Wyoming?
4. Which state is nicknamed the Buckeye State?
5. President Harry S Truman often played his state song on the piano. Name that tune.
6. What is Arizona's state tree?
7. Deseret is the former name of what state?
8. What state song is named for a river within the state?

6 QUESTIONS:

1. What's the name of the world's largest canyon and where is it located?
2. Michigan is famous for building more of these than any other state. What are these products?
3. What is the state bird of New Mexico?
4. When this song was adopted as a state song, Ray Charles sang it to the state assembly. What was the song?
5. Name four of the eight states which border Tennessee.
6. What is the capital city of North Dakota?
7. The first college founded in America in 1636 is located in the state of Massachusetts. Name the college.
8. What is the state bird of Utah?

7 QUESTIONS:

1. Thomas A. Edison, famous for inventing the incandescent electric light, was born in which midwestern state?
2. Which state is nicknamed the Keystone State?
3. What are the only two state capitals to be named for the state they're in?
4. At 242 feet below sea level, where is the lowest geographical point in the U.S.?
5. Name Wisconsin's state bird.
6. Hot dogs, ice cream cones, and Cracker Jack were all thought up in this state. Name the state.
7. Which is the smallest state in the U.S.?
8. Which state is nicknamed the Hawkeye State?

8 QUESTIONS:

1. What famous song was written at Baltimore's Fort McH_____ _____ the War of 1812?
2. What is the state flc of Washington?
3. What is the only sta of two words that it of two words?
4. Where is the only r United States locat
5. What is the only U. just one other statt
6. What is the only st by four of the five (Superior, Lake Mic Lake Huron, Lake Lake Ontario.)
7. What four state ca "city" in their name
8. What section of the United States gives its name to a popular type of chowder?

1. Boise
2. The yellowhammer
3. The violet
4. Tuscumbia, Alabama
5. Indiana
6. Alaska
7. Florida
8. The Statue of Liberty

1. Arizona
2. Tennessee
3. New York
4. Kansas
5. Vermont
6. Alaska
7. California
8. Texas

8 ANSWERS:

1. "The Star-Spangled Banner"
2. The rhododendron
3. Santa Fe, New Mexico
4. Honolulu, Hawaii
5. Maine, which borders New Hampshire
6. Michigan
7. Carson City, Nevada; Jefferson City, Missouri; Oklahoma City, Oklahoma; and Salt Lake City, Utah
8. New England

7 ANSWERS:

1. Ohio
2. Pennsylvania
3. Oklahoma City, Oklahoma and Indianapolis, Indiana
4. Death Valley, California
5. The robin
6. Ohio
7. Rhode Island
8. Iowa

1. Madison, Wisconsin; Jackson, Mississippi; Jefferson City, Missouri; and Lincoln, Nebraska
2. Michigan
3. Pennsylvania and New Jersey
4. Hawaii
5. "Carry Me Back To Old Virginny"
6. Trenton, New Jersey
7. Massachusetts
8. "Oklahoma"

6 ANSWERS:

1. The Grand Canyon in Arizona
2. Cars and trucks
3. The roadrunner
4. "Georgia On My Mind"
5. North Carolina, Georgia, Alabama, Mississippi, Arkansas, Missouri, Kentucky, and Virginia
6. Bismarck
7. Harvard
8. The sea gull

1. Missouri
2. Alaska
3. Arkansas
4. "I Love You, California"
5. Arkansas, Illinois, Iowa, Kansas, Kentucky, Nebraska, Oklahoma, and Tennessee
6. Connecticut
7. Pennsylvania
8. Florida

5 ANSWERS:

1. Baltimore oriole
2. Kentucky
3. Cheyenne
4. Ohio
5. The "Missouri Waltz"
6. The Palo Verde
7. Utah
8. "Swanee River" in Florida

1. What's West Virginia's number-one export?
2. What's Vermont's state flower?
3. This U.S. state ends with a G.
4. Where are the largest operating gold mines in the Western Hemisphere located?
5. Montana is Spanish for what English word?
6. What's the capital of Missouri?
7. What's the state tree of Mississippi?
8. What three presidents named John were born in Massachusetts?

16 QUESTIONS:

1. Name the state bird of New Jersey.
2. The Cowboy Capital of America is in which town in Kansas?
3. Which was the last colony to become a state?
4. What's the capital of Texas?
5. Rhode Island is an island. True or False.
6. Name four of the eight U.S. Presidents born in Virginia.
7. What present-day holiday did the Pilgrims introduce in America?
8. What is the world's first and largest U.S. national park?

1. What's the state tree of North Dakota?
2. What famous waterfall does the U.S. share with Canada?
3. Which U.S. lake has the most salty water?
4. What is the capital of Virginia?
5. The sun shines 20 hours a day in Alaska during which season?
6. Where do you see the most stars?
7. What was the first state that allowed women the right to vote?
8. In 1882, Wisconsin was the site of the debut circus show of what famous brothers?

15 QUESTIONS:

1. What is Indiana's state bird?
2. What's the capital of Michigan?
3. The Pilgrims landed here in 1620.
4. What's the capital of Kansas?
5. This state produces more wooden toothpicks than any other (about 100 million a day).
6. Canton, Ohio is the home of this pro sport's hall of fame.
7. What's the state flower of New York?
8. Which state receives the least amount of rainfall?

1. Dorothy in *The Wizard of Oz* came from which U.S. state?
2. The famous Fulton Fish Market is located in which U.S. city?
3. This state is all wet. In all the world the most rainfall is recorded here.
4. Delaware's state bird has a color in its name. What color?
5. The state of Texas could fit into the state of Alaska how many times?
6. Name the biggest lake in the U.S.
7. What is Wisconsin's state tree?
8. In 1581 the first U.S. roadway was built in what state?

1. At 1,932 feet, Crater Lake is the deepest lake in the U.S. It's located at the top of an inactive volcano in what state?
2. The Wright brothers are famous for making the world's first successful airplane flight in what U.S. state?
3. Which of the Great Lakes has the world's longest freshwater beach?
4. What is South Carolina's state flower?
5. In 1846, Hoboken, New Jersey was the site of the world's first professional game in what sport?
6. What farm product does Kansas produce more of than any other state?
7. Which is the only U.S. city with a glacier?
8. What's the state bird of Maine?

13 QUESTIONS:

1. What is the capital of Maryland?
2. Before 1819 Maine used to be a part of what state?
3. In 1935 the first *night* professional baseball game was played in what city and state?
4. Name five of the thirteen original states.
5. Where is Angel Island located?
6. Which U.S. *city* is the most populated?
7. Iowa has the largest packing plant of what favorite movie food?
8. The mail in Santa Claus, Indiana increases tremendously during what holiday season?

14 QUESTIONS:

1. Name the 39th U.S. President, who was born in Georgia.
2. Which is located in Anaheim, California, Disneyland, or Disney World?
3. The town of Enterprise, Alabama erected a statue of what cotton-pickin' insect?
4. The heads of how many U.S. Presidents are carved in stone in the Mount Rushmore National Memorial in South Dakota?
5. Bone remains of what age-old animals can still be viewed in Utah?
6. What's Connecticut's state tree?
7. Hawaii is the only U.S. state that grows this kind of beans.
8. This was the site of the 1984 Summer Olympic Games.

12 ANSWERS:

1. Coal
2. The red clover
3. Wyoming
4. South Dakota
5. Mountain
6. Jefferson City
7. The magnolia
8. John Adams, John Quincy Adams, and John F. Kennedy

ANSWERS:

1. The American elm
2. Niagara Falls
3. The Great Salt Lake in Utah
4. Richmond
5. Summer
6. Hollywood, California
7. Wyoming
8. The Ringling brothers

ANSWERS:

1. Oregon
2. North Carolina (Kitty Hawk)
3. Lake Huron
4. The yellow jessamine
5. Baseball
6. Wheat
7. Boulder, Colorado
8. The chickadee

16 ANSWERS:

1. The Eastern goldfinch
2. Dodge City
3. Rhode Island
4. Austin
5. False
6. George Washington, Thomas Jefferson, James Madison, James Monroe, William Henry Harrison, John Tyler, Zachary Taylor, and Woodrow Wilson
7. Thanksgiving
8. Yellowstone Park in Wyoming

15 ANSWERS:

1. The cardinal
2. Lansing
3. Plymouth, Massachusetts
4. Topeka
5. Maine
6. Professional Football Hall of Fame
7. The rose
8. Nevada

14 ANSWERS:

1. Jimmy Carter
2. Disneyland
3. The boll weevil
4. Four: Washington, Jefferson, Lincoln, and Theodore Roosevelt.
5. Dinosaurs
6. The white oak
7. Coffee
8. Los Angeles, California

13 ANSWERS:

1. Annapolis
2. Massachusetts
3. Cincinnati, Ohio
4. Georgia, S. Carolina, N. Carolina, Delaware, Maryland, Virginia, Pennsylvania, New Jersey, New York, New Hampshire, Massachusetts, Rhode Island, and Connecticut
5. In San Francisco Bay
6. New York City
7. Popcorn
8. Christmas

ANSWERS:

1. Kansas
2. New York
3. Hawaii (Mt. Waialeale on Kauai),
4. Blue——the blue hen chicken
5. Two times
6. Lake Superior
7. The sugar maple
8. New Mexico, El Camino Real

AL ALABAMA
CAPITAL CITY	Montgomery
STATE FLOWER	Camellia
STATE BIRD	Yellowhammer

AK ALASKA
CAPITAL CITY	Juneau
STATE FLOWER	Forget-me-not
STATE BIRD	Willow ptarmigan

AZ ARIZONA
CAPITAL CITY	Phoenix
STATE FLOWER	Saguaro cactus
STATE BIRD	Cactus wren

AR ARKANSAS
CAPITAL CITY	Little Rock
STATE FLOWER	Apple blossom
STATE BIRD	Mockingbird

CA CALIFORNIA
CAPITAL CITY	Sacramento
STATE FLOWER	Golden poppy
STATE BIRD	California valley quail

CO COLORADO
CAPITAL CITY	Denver
STATE FLOWER	Rocky Mountain columbine
STATE BIRD	Lark bunting

CT CONNECTICUT
CAPITAL CITY	Hartford
STATE FLOWER	Mountain laurel
STATE BIRD	Robin

DE DELAWARE
CAPITAL CITY	Dover
STATE FLOWER	Peach blossom
STATE BIRD	Blue hen chicken

FL FLORIDA
CAPITAL CITY	Tallahassee
STATE FLOWER	Orange blossom
STATE BIRD	Mockingbird

GA GEORGIA
CAPITAL CITY	Atlanta
STATE FLOWER	Cherokee rose
STATE BIRD	Brown thrasher

HI HAWAII
CAPITAL CITY	Honolulu
STATE FLOWER	Hibiscus
STATE BIRD	Nene (Hawaiian goose)

ID IDAHO
CAPITAL CITY	Boise
STATE FLOWER	Syringa
STATE BIRD	Mountain bluebird

IL ILLINOIS
CAPITAL CITY	Springfield
STATE FLOWER	Violet
STATE BIRD	Cardinal

IN INDIANA
CAPITAL CITY	Indianapolis
STATE FLOWER	Peony
STATE BIRD	Cardinal

IA IOWA
CAPITAL CITY	Des Moines
STATE FLOWER	Wild rose
STATE BIRD	Eastern goldfinch

KS KANSAS
CAPITAL CITY	Topeka
STATE FLOWER	Sunflower
STATE BIRD	Western meadowlark

KY KENTUCKY
CAPITAL CITY	Frankfort
STATE FLOWER	Goldenrod
STATE BIRD	Cardinal

LA LOUISIANA
CAPITAL CITY	Baton Rouge
STATE FLOWER	Magnolia
STATE BIRD	Brown pelican

ME MAINE
CAPITAL CITY	Augusta
STATE FLOWER	White pine cone and tassel
STATE BIRD	Chickadee

MD MARYLAND
CAPITAL CITY	Annapolis
STATE FLOWER	Black-eyed Susan
STATE BIRD	Baltimore oriole

MA MASSACHUSETTS
CAPITAL CITY	Boston
STATE FLOWER	Mayflower
STATE BIRD	Chickadee

MI MICHIGAN
CAPITAL CITY	Lansing
STATE FLOWER	Apple blossom
STATE BIRD	Robin

MN MINNESOTA
CAPITAL CITY	St. Paul
STATE FLOWER	Showy lady's slipper
STATE BIRD	Common loon

MS MISSISSIPPI
CAPITAL CITY	Jackson
STATE FLOWER	Magnolia
STATE BIRD	Mockingbird

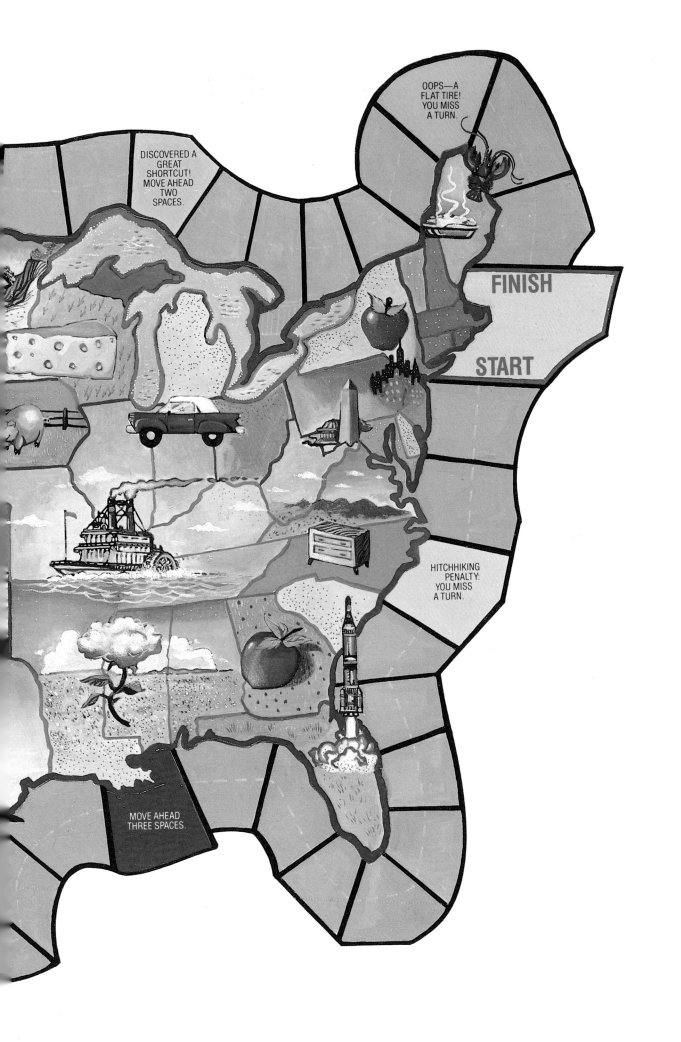

MO MISSOURI
CAPITAL CITY	Jefferson City
STATE FLOWER	Hawthorn
STATE BIRD	Bluebird

MT MONTANA
CAPITAL CITY	Helena
STATE FLOWER	Bitterroot
STATE BIRD	Western meadowlark

NE NEBRASKA
CAPITAL CITY	Lincoln
STATE FLOWER	Goldenrod
STATE BIRD	Western meadowlark

NV NEVADA
CAPITAL CITY	Carson City
STATE FLOWER	Sagebrush
STATE BIRD	Mountain bluebird

NH NEW HAMPSHIRE
CAPITAL CITY	Concord
STATE FLOWER	Purple lilac
STATE BIRD	Purple finch

NJ NEW JERSEY
CAPITAL CITY	Trenton
STATE FLOWER	Purple violet
STATE BIRD	Eastern goldfinch

NM NEW MEXICO
CAPITAL CITY	Santa Fe
STATE FLOWER	Yucca
STATE BIRD	Roadrunner

NY NEW YORK
CAPITAL CITY	Albany
STATE FLOWER	Rose
STATE BIRD	Bluebird

NC NORTH CAROLINA
CAPITAL CITY	Raleigh
STATE FLOWER	Dogwood
STATE BIRD	Cardinal

ND NORTH DAKOTA
CAPITAL CITY	Bismarck
STATE FLOWER	Wild prairie rose
STATE BIRD	Western meadowlark

OH OHIO
CAPITAL CITY	Columbus
STATE FLOWER	Scarlet carnation
STATE BIRD	Cardinal

OK OKLAHOMA
CAPITAL CITY	Oklahoma City
STATE FLOWER	Mistletoe
STATE BIRD	Scissor-tailed flycatcher

OR OREGON
CAPITAL CITY	Salem
STATE FLOWER	Oregon grape
STATE BIRD	Western meadowlark

PA PENNSYLVANIA
CAPITAL CITY	Harrisburg
STATE FLOWER	Mountain laurel
STATE BIRD	Ruffed grouse

RI RHODE ISLAND
CAPITAL CITY	Providence
STATE FLOWER	Violet
STATE BIRD	Rhode Island red

SC SOUTH CAROLINA
CAPITAL CITY	Columbia
STATE FLOWER	Yellow jessamine
STATE BIRD	Carolina wren

SD SOUTH DAKOTA
CAPITAL CITY	Pierre
STATE FLOWER	Pasqueflower
STATE BIRD	Ring-necked pheasant

TN TENNESSEE
CAPITAL CITY	Nashville
STATE FLOWER	Iris
STATE BIRD	Mockingbird

TX TEXAS
CAPITAL CITY	Austin
STATE FLOWER	Bluebonnet
STATE BIRD	Mockingbird

UT UTAH
CAPITAL CITY	Salt Lake City
STATE FLOWER	Sego lily
STATE BIRD	Sea gull

VT VERMONT
CAPITAL CITY	Montpelier
STATE FLOWER	Red clover
STATE BIRD	Hermit thrush

VA VIRGINIA
CAPITAL CITY	Richmond
STATE FLOWER	Flowering dogwood
STATE BIRD	Cardinal

WA WASHINGTON
CAPITAL CITY	Olympia
STATE FLOWER	Rhododendron
STATE BIRD	Willow goldfinch

WV WEST VIRGINIA
CAPITAL CITY	Charleston
STATE FLOWER	Rhododendron
STATE BIRD	Cardinal

WI WISCONSIN
CAPITAL CITY	Madison
STATE FLOWER	Wood violet
STATE BIRD	Robin

WY WYOMING
CAPITAL CITY	Cheyenne
STATE FLOWER	Indian paintbrush
STATE BIRD	Meadowlark

1. What is the northernmost state?
2. Which state is nicknamed the Lone Star State?
3. What is the capital of Alabama?
4. In which state is Niagara Falls located?
5. What New York City borough has the largest Greek population?
6. Which city is nicknamed the Windy City?
7. Which U.S. city is known as the chocolate capital of the world?
8. What is the capital of Utah?

24 QUESTIONS:

1. The Empire State Building can be found in what city?
2. Where can you find the Liberty Bell?
3. Which states have the violet as their state flower?
4. Which state is nicknamed the Cotton State?
5. Dover is the capital of which state?
6. In what state can the volcano Mt. St. Helens be found?
7. The Indians called this Great Lake, Gitchigumi.
8. In what state is the Mardi Gras held?

QUESTIONS:

1. What city is nicknamed Beantown?
2. The U.S. capital is Washington, D.C. What does D.C. mean?
3. Hollywood is the name of a city in which two states?
4. Name a state starting with the letter G.
5. Where is the Baseball Hall of Fame?
6. What is located at 1600 Pennsylvania Avenue?
7. Name the large river forming part of the U.S.–Mexican border?
8. What is the longest river in the United States?

23 QUESTIONS:

1. What city is nicknamed the City of Brotherly Love?
2. Which state in the midwest has the most underground caves?
3. Which two U.S. states end with the letter Y?
4. Where can you find Pearl Harbor?
5. Daniel Boone, Kit Carson, and Muhammad Ali were all born in which state?
6. The famous Gateway Arch can be found in what city and state?
7. How many state names start with the word "new"?
8. Which state is known as the Garden State?

QUESTIONS:

1. Which state is closest to the Soviet Union?
2. Which U.S. state grows the most sugarcane?
3. Where would you find the "National Hollerin' Contest"?
4. Which state is made up of islands?
5. The world's busiest airport, O'Hare, can be found in which city and state?
6. Which state has more lakes than any other state?
7. Abraham Lincoln grew up in which state?
8. Where can you find the world's largest baseball bat factory?

21 QUESTIONS:

1. Where was the United States capital when George Washington was inaugurated as President?
2. Which cities are nicknamed the Twin Cities?
3. In which state is the Petrified Forest National Park found?
4. What is the capital of Louisiana?
5. What is the state flower of Massachusetts?
6. In which state did surfing begin?
7. How many states border the Pacific Ocean?
8. Pierre is the capital of which state?

22 QUESTIONS:

1. Which state is directly north of Oregon?
2. What state begins and ends with the letter O?
3. The city of Fairbanks is located in what U.S. state?
4. There is a North Carolina and a South Carolina. Name another North/South pair.
5. The Uncle Remus Museum is in which Southern state?
6. What is the state bird of Connecticut?
7. What time is it in California if it's noon in New York?
8. Where can the city of Toledo be found?

1. Alaska
2. Texas
3. Montgomery
4. New York
5. Queens
6. Chicago
7. Hershey, Pennsylvania
8. Salt Lake City

1. Boston, Massachusetts
2. District of Columbia
3. California and Florida
4. Georgia
5. Cooperstown, New York
6. The White House
7. The Rio Grande
8. The Mississippi

24 ANSWERS:

1. New York City
2. Philadelphia, Pennsylvania
3. Rhode Island, Illinois, and Wisconsin
4. Alabama
5. Delaware
6. Washington
7. Lake Superior
8. Louisiana

23 ANSWERS:

1. Philadelphia
2. Missouri
3. Kentucky and New Jersey
4. Hawaii
5. Kentucky
6. St. Louis, Missouri
7. Four: New Hampshire, New Jersey, New Mexico, and New York
8. New Jersey

22 ANSWERS:

1. Washington
2. Ohio
3. Alaska
4. North Dakota and South Dakota
5. Georgia
6. Robin
7. 9 A.M.
8. Ohio

1. Hawaii
2. Texas
3. Michigan
4. Arizona, New Mexico, Utah, and
5. Colorado
6. Kentucky
7. Alaska
8. New York

1. Alaska
2. Hawaii
3. Spivey's Corners, North Carolina
4. Hawaii
5. Chicago, Illinois
6. Florida
7. Indiana
8. Kentucky

21 ANSWERS:

1. New York City
2. Minneapolis and St. Paul, Minnesot
3. Arizona
4. Baton Rouge
5. Mayflower
6. Hawaii
7. Five: Alaska, Washington, Oregon, California, and Hawaii
8. South Dakota

1. Where is the Miss America Pageant held every year?
2. A chicken is the mascot for which baseball team in California?
3. What is the capital of Vermont?
4. Where is the Rose Bowl held?
5. What Arizona city got its name from a flag that was flown from a pine tree?
6. Name the highest mountain in the United States.
7. What does the abbreviation ME stand for?
8. What is the capital of Nebraska?

---

1. What large lake can be found on the border between California and Nevada?
2. Name the capital of Wisconsin.
3. What is the state bird of Wyoming?
4. This New York canal runs from Buffalo to Albany.
5. In what state is Disney World located?
6. In what state is Yankee Stadium located?
7. What is the capital of Rhode Island?
8. Name the four chains of mountains that can be found in the western U.S.

---

32 QUESTIONS:

1. Where can you find Cape Canaveral?
2. How many islands make up the state of Hawaii?
3. Name the capital of Nevada.
4. Name the two states located directly north of Florida.
5. Crystal City, Texas, the Spinach Capital of the World, erected a statue of what famous cartoon character?
6. What ocean can be found off the east coast of the U.S.?
7. In which state was gold discovered in 1849?
8. What is the capital of Kentucky?

---

1. Name the large chain of mountains found in the eastern U.S.
2. President Abraham Lincoln delivered his Gettysburg Address in what state?
3. This river runs along the full length of Tennessee's western border.
4. Name the capital of New Hampshire.
5. In which state is Big Sur located?
6. Where was the first Thanksgiving held?
7. What city is nicknamed Motown?
8. Where can you find the Grand Old Opry—the home of country-western music?

---

31 QUESTIONS:

1. Where can you find London Bridge?
2. What is the name of the large body of water that is located between Florida and Texas?
3. What river did Huckleberry Finn travel on?
4. What is a peninsula?
5. This California desert is nicknamed High Desert. What's its official name?
6. What is the capital of Florida?
7. How many different time zones are there in the continental U.S.?
8. Which ocean is located off the west coast of the U.S.?

---

30 QUESTIONS:

1. If you wanted to visit the Smithsonian Institute, which city would you have to go to?
2. Which state is nicknamed the Centennial State?
3. Where is the Lincoln Memorial?
4. What is the world's longest bridge and where can it be found?
5. What is the tallest tree in the United States?
6. Name the capital of Oregon.
7. What is the state song of Wyoming?
8. Where can you find the Vietnam Veterans' Memorial?

---

1. The 1933 World's Fair was held in this city.
2. Which city claims that it holds the largest Thanksgiving Day Parade?
3. Name the state with the smallest population.
4. What is the capital of Pennsylvania?
5. Which city is nicknamed the Mile-High City?
6. Which state has the second largest land area?
7. Okefenokee is one of the largest swamps in the U.S. Where can you find it?
8. Which state is known as Home of the Indians?

---

29 QUESTIONS:

1. What bridge links San Francisco and Marin County, California?
2. What is the capital of Ohio?
3. The abbreviation ID stands for which state?
4. The beginning of the American Revolution started in which two Massachusetts cities?
5. License plates in this New England state carry the word "Vacationland."
6. Where is the U.S. Air Force Academy located?
7. Where will you find Yellowstone National Park?
8. The hibiscus is the state flower of which state?

ANSWERS:

1. Atlantic City, New Jersey
2. The San Diego Padres
3. Montpelier
4. Pasadena, California
5. Flagstaff, Arizona
6. Mount McKinley in Alaska
7. Maine
8. Lincoln

---

32 ANSWERS:

1. Florida
2. Eight
3. Carson City
4. Alabama and Georgia
5. Popeye
6. Atlantic
7. California
8. Frankfort

ANSWERS:

1. Lake Tahoe
2. Madison
3. Meadowlark
4. The Erie Canal
5. Florida
6. New York
7. Providence
8. The Rocky Mountains, the Sierra Nevada, the Cascades, and the Coast Range

---

31 ANSWERS:

1. Arizona
2. The Gulf of Mexico
3. The Mississippi
4. An area of land with water on three sides
5. The Mojave Desert
6. Tallahassee
7. Four
8. Pacific

ANSWERS:

1. The Appalachian
2. Pennsylvania
3. The Mississippi
4. Concord
5. California
6. Plymouth, Massachusetts
7. Detroit, Michigan
8. Nashville, Tennessee

---

30 ANSWERS:

1. Washington, D.C.
2. Colorado
3. Washington, D.C.
4. The Verrazano Narrows Bridge in New York
5. The redwood
6. Salem
7. "Wyoming"
8. Washington, D.C.

ANSWERS:

1. Chicago
2. New York City
3. Alaska
4. Harrisburg
5. Denver
6. Texas
7. Georgia
8. Oklahoma

---

29 ANSWERS:

1. The Golden Gate Bridge
2. Columbus
3. Idaho
4. Lexington and Concord
5. Maine
6. Colorado Springs, Colorado
7. Wyoming
8. Hawaii